The 2010 San Francisco Giants incredible run to their first World Series Championship!

Sport Publishing

President: Phil Saran
Editor-in-Chief: Tom Zenner
Chief Designer: Kelley Ellert
Senior Writer: David Cooper
Senior Writer: Brad Botkin
VP Sales & Distribution: Don Kapral
Web Designer: Aaron Garza
Editorial Assistant: Shondasha Vana
Operations Director: Ryan Saran
Research Coordinator: Brooke Zenner
Photo Editor: Lindsay Saran, Brent Herrin
Photos Provided By: AP Images
Printed By: Dome Printing

ISBN: 978 0 9831180 1 5
UPC: 0 74470 25941 1 03

This book is available in quantity at special discounts for your group or organization.

For further information, contact the publisher.

Printed in the United States

Sports Publishing, LLC
www.sfgiantsworldchamps.com

BEARD 1
TEXAS 0
Bank of America

CONTENTS

A Season of Destiny Takes Shape
2010 Spring Training

A Summer To Remember
2010 Giants Regular Season

Making History
Giants vs Braves 2010 NLDS

Shocking the World
Giants vs Phillies 2010 NLCS

Classic Ending!
Giants vs Rangers 2010 World Series

Picture Perfect
Giants 2010 Photo Gallery

N.L.
WESTERN
DIVISION
CHAMPIONS
SAN FRANCISCO
GIANTS
CROIX DE CANDLESTICK
VENI · VIDI · VIXI
FIRST WIN!
WORLD SERIES
2002
GIANTS
YES WE
CANNABIS
YES ON 19

FOREWORD

Do you remember the last time the Giants celebrated a World Series Championship in San Francisco? Of course you don't, it's never happened. Since leaving New York 52 years ago the Giants have provided their loyal fan base a lot of thrills and excitement, but never have they ended a baseball season the envy of the Major Leagues. And to put it mildly, Giants' fans have never had a team like this to follow either. Call them quirky. Eccentric. Maybe even a little bit weird, but from now until the end of time you'll also be calling the 2010 Giants World Champs. Rarely has a team gelled like this masterfully assembled collection of superstars, role players, grinders, gamers and goof balls.

And as we all witnessed, this was not a fluke. The Braves saw their manager and playoff dreams permanently retired. The Phillies didn't phlop, they were phlattened, by Giants pitching that was borderline masterful. As for the Texas Rangers, well, they really do things big in Texas, including lose.

You've waited a long time for this Giants fans. As talented as this team is, it could possibly be the beginning of a Bay Area dynasty. Then again, it might be a one-time joyride that should be enjoyed and cherished for at least the next 52 years or so.

T. Z.

Tom Zenner
Editor in Chief
Sport Publishing, LLC

DIAMOND
SAFEWAY
Coors LIGHT
CHW
PlayStation
WORLD SERIES
charles SCHWAB
YAHOO!
VISA
TOYOTA
State Farm

A Season of Destiny Takes Shape

2010 Spring Training

Considering the Giants hadn't won a World Series since 1954, way back when the team was still playing in New York and Willie Mays was making that timeless, over-the-shoulder catch, it would be a stretch to say anyone was expecting a championship run in 2010. But still, as the Giants embarked upon Cactus League play in Arizona, there was a palpable buzz—if only in a cautiously optimistic sort of way—pervading the most beautiful city in the world. Even the most casual fan could feel it. This team had a new identity. It had been in the works for a few years, but in 2010, the feeling around the city, and around baseball in general, was that the Barry Bonds era was finally fading out.

Giant fans were no longer thinking about tainted records and court cases. They were thinking about the best young pitching staff in baseball. They were thinking about a long-haired, rubber-armed righty named Tim Lincecum. They were thinking about the most anonymous stud pitcher in baseball, Matt Cain, who had been carving up opposing teams' lineups in the shadow of Lincecum's multiple Cy Young trophies. They were thinking about a fire-balling closer named Brian Wilson. And if for no other reason than those three names, San Franciscans had hope.

ANCHOR STEAM
BEER
ME

Having said that, there were still a lot of questions surrounding this team. Could they hit? Was the bullpen going to hold up? Was Edgar Renteria still a serviceable every-day shortstop? Giant fans are a famously intelligent bunch, and they knew these were real questions. If the Giants were going to contend in an extremely tough, evenly matched National League West, where the Rockies and Dodgers had reined supreme a year ago, they definitely had their work cut out for them.

For starters, they would be depending on a mix of veterans like the Juan Uribe and Aaron Rowand and Bengie Molina, along with the fan favorite Pablo Sandoval, a.k.a. the "Kung Fu Panda," who was the team's lone consistent offensive threat in 2009. There was also the newly acquired Aubrey Huff, upon whom general manager Brian Sabean was depending to have a bounce-back year. Come January, Huff

wasn't even on a roster. Nobody knew it at the time, but that would become the theme of the Giants entire season—Guys nobody else wanted.

Sabean also brought in the widely respected Mark DeRosa, a known winner and a guy who could potentially fill a lot of holes with his versatility. But again, cautious optimism was the theme of the pre-season. With young, lively arms like the aforementioned Lincecum and Cain, anything was possible. But would that be enough? After all, they had those guys last year, and still, they only finished in third place. 88 victories is nothing to be ashamed of, but at the end of the day, San Francisco wanted a title.

After all, as mentioned earlier, the Giants hadn't finished on top of the baseball world since 1954,

behind only the cursed Cubs and the historically horrible Indians. And the Giants were starting to feel cursed too, starting with the Earthquake Series in 1989. In that year, the Giants had to face two of the toughest pitchers in baseball in Oakland's Dave Stewart and Bob Welch. Then, after the earthquake gave them an extended break, the Giants had to face those two guys again in Games 3 and 4.

And every Giant fan remembers 2002. Scott Spezio. The title was all but wrapped up, the champagne corks ready to pop. Then, disaster. Everything spirals, the Angels and the ridiculous Rally Monkey stage a furious comeback. They win Game 6. Game 7. And just like that, the drought continues. Players don't think about that kind of stuff. Heck, not a single guy from that 2002 team was still on the Giants' roster. But rest assured, fans think about it all the time. Just ask the folks in Boston. The players might say things like, "the past has nothing to do with us" and "this is a new year, a new team." But fans' memories are long.

So the team broke for Arizona with the endless possibilities of a new season in front of them. The general consensus was that they were good, but not great. They weren't old, but they weren't young. They were, in a word, unpredictable. They could finish in the middle of the pack or they could run away with the division. Anything could happen. It's like they say: That's why they play the game.

GIANTS

Numbers Game

Giants 2009 Record
88-74 (3rd in NL West)

657 Total Runs Scored
611 Total Runs Allowed

2009 Home Attendance
2,682,110 (7th in National League)

A SUMMER TO REMEMBER

2010 Giants Regular Season

REGULAR SEASON 92-70

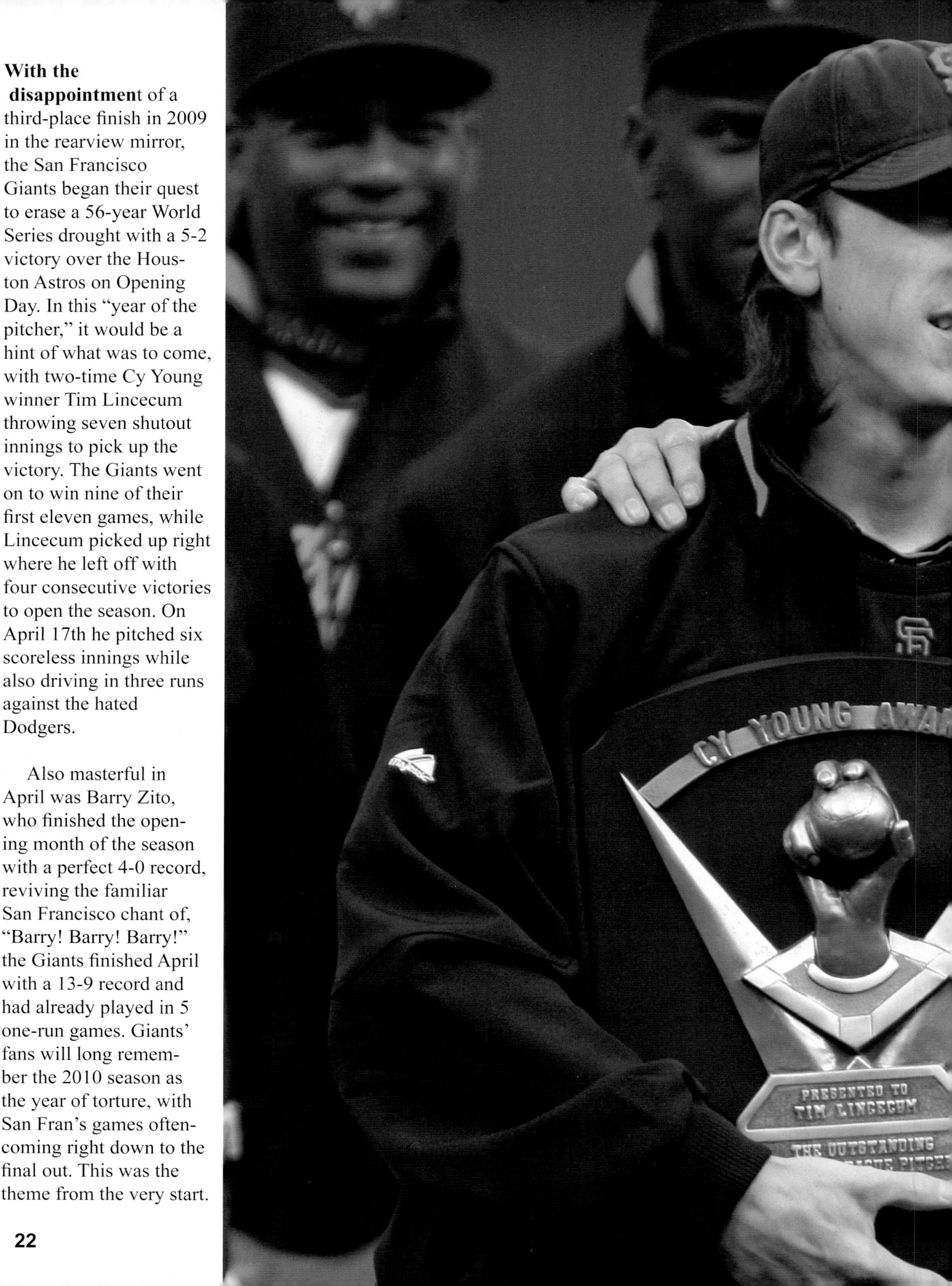

With the disappointment of a third-place finish in 2009 in the rearview mirror, the San Francisco Giants began their quest to erase a 56-year World Series drought with a 5-2 victory over the Houston Astros on Opening Day. In this "year of the pitcher," it would be a hint of what was to come, with two-time Cy Young winner Tim Lincecum throwing seven shutout innings to pick up the victory. The Giants went on to win nine of their first eleven games, while Lincecum picked up right where he left off with four consecutive victories to open the season. On April 17th he pitched six scoreless innings while also driving in three runs against the hated Dodgers.

Also masterful in April was Barry Zito, who finished the opening month of the season with a perfect 4-0 record, reviving the familiar San Francisco chant of, "Barry! Barry! Barry!" the Giants finished April with a 13-9 record and had already played in 5 one-run games. Giants' fans will long remember the 2010 season as the year of torture, with San Fran's games often-coming right down to the final out. This was the theme from the very start.

CY YOUNG AWARD
PRESENTED TO

As the season rolled toward the dog days of summer the Giants were still filling holes, trying to find the right lineup, with Bruce Bochy scribbling out different lineup card almost every day. Mark DeRosa was playing left field one day and second base the next. Juan Uribe could be anywhere in the infield on any given day. Nate Schierholtz was playing right field, then Jay Bowker was out there. One day Aaron Rowand was in center, and the next day Andres Torres was patrolling the middle outfield spot. And all the while, the Padres were off and running. The Giants hadn't started out badly, but still, they were in chase mode right off the bat. And then, on May 29th, a rookie by the name of Buster Posey made his Major League debut. And for all intents and purposes, that's when the run to the World Series started.

After playing in a minor league game the night before, all Posey did in his first big league game was collect three hits and three RBIs, and in the process, make hitting Major League pitching look laughably easy.

OAK
TEX
DET
TOR
BOS

Levi's
CLE
KC
CIN
PIT
PHI
COL
LA
AZ
at&t
365

"What a great job the kid did," said manager Bruce Bochy of Posey's breakout performance in the Giants' 12-1 victory over the Arizona Diamondbacks. "I'm sure he didn't get much sleep last night, then he goes out and gets big hits for us. We needed it."

He was right. Posey was just the spark the Giants needed. The next night he collected three more hits as Andres Torres sent the Giants to an extra-inning win with a walk-off single in the tenth. Torres—a career journeyman who'd never had a secured position in the Big Leagues, a guy who'd been a minor league free agent five different times since being taken in the 4th round of the 1998 draft by the Detroit Tigers—was starting to assert himself. And although nobody realized it at the time, he was fast becoming the model of the 2010 Giants.

Nobody else wanted him. The Giants took him. And they never looked back.

In mid-June the Giants began interleague play with four straight wins, including a three-game sweep over their cross-bay rival. But as will often happen in baseball, things took a sudden and dramatic turn for the worse when the Giants fell to the Boston Red Sox 4-2 on June 26th, which marked the beginning of a seven-game losing streak, the longest the team had endured since 2007. The loss in that red Sox game was credited to

Madison Bumgarner, who had been called up from Triple A Fresno to make the start in Fenway Park. Suffice it to say, things would get better for the lanky lefty.

The Giants wound up recovering nicely from that losing streak, proceeding to win 16 of their next 20 games, capped off by yet another one-run, extra-inning win over the Diamondbacks. Buster Posey was on fire during this stretch, tearing up National League pitching to the tune of an 18-game hitting streak, passing Orlando Cepeda for the second-longest hitting streak by a Giants rookie. On July 27th, in a 6-4 victory over the Florida Marlins, Posey stretched his hitting streak to 20 games, leaving him just two shy of the team record of 22, set by Willie McCovey in 1959. Closer Brian Wilson recorded his 29th save in 31 chances, and the Giants pulled to within 2 ½ games of the division-leading Padres. Edgar Renteria was starting to like the team's chances.

"That's why I signed (here)," Renteria said. "I knew (the Giants) had a lot of talent. Last year it didn't work out, but this year we have a chance to do it. We're going to be ready."

Things were starting to take shape.

Even though Tim Lincecum went through a stretch where he lost his mechanics, and in doing so, lost five straight decisions, the Giants were starting to establish what they were all about. This team never had an ego, but as the season progressed, this was becoming more and more evident. Everybody was embracing their roles, picking up the slack when-

GIA
A2000

URIBE
5
NATIONALS
PNC
Official Bank of the Nationals
Coca-Cola
GIANTS
ROWAND
F. SANCHEZ
HUFF
POSEY
URIBE
ISHIKAWA
SANDOVAL
SCHIERHOLTZ
J. SANCHEZ
BUSTER POSEY
MAXWELL
GUZMAN
ZIMMERMAN
DUNN
WILLINGHAM
RODRIGUEZ
MORSE
DESMOND
STAMMEN
Giants
Nationals
GEICO
NATIONAL LEAGUE
AMERICAN LEAGUE

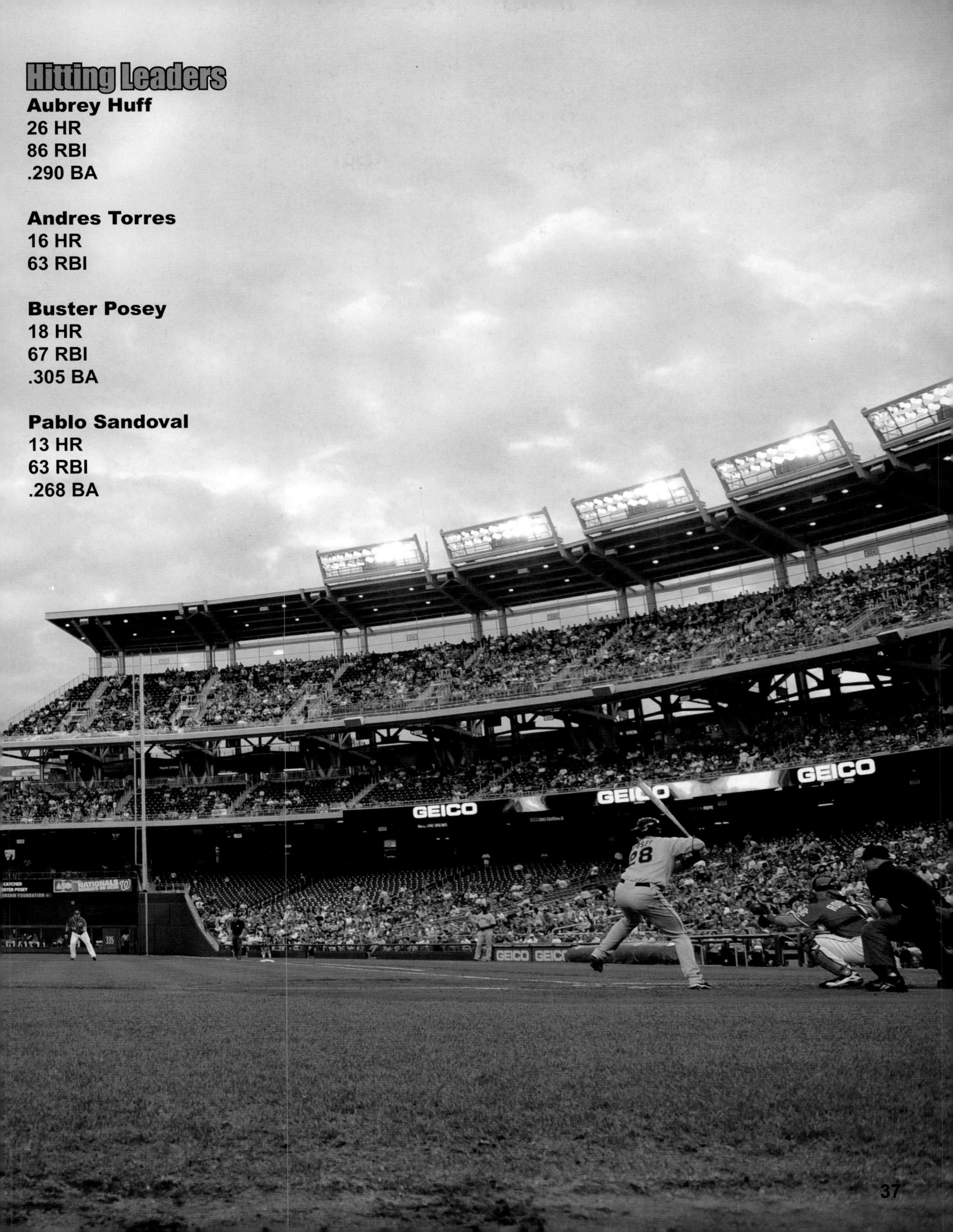

Hitting Leaders

Aubrey Huff
26 HR
86 RBI
.290 BA

Andres Torres
16 HR
63 RBI

Buster Posey
18 HR
67 RBI
.305 BA

Pablo Sandoval
13 HR
63 RBI
.268 BA

ever and however the team needed—guys like Pablo Sandoval (who was coming of a year in which he hit .330 and 25 homers, only to find major struggles in 2010) cheering for their teammates when they weren't in the lineup. Bruce Bochy had made an unspoken statement that hew as going to play the guys that gave the team the best chance to win. Renteria was on the bench. Rowand was on the bench. Guys were playing in different places every day. And the city was starting to fall in love with their team. "The misfits," they called them. "The cast-offs."

And nobody fit that role better than Cody Ross.

GIANTS

Make Your Own
Lou Seal
FAN LOT
GIANTS

23
BRACAMONTE
85

SWEEP
LA

ROCKIES

In a move largely thought to be as much about blocking the Padres (who the Giants were still trying to catch in the NL West), San Francisco claimed Ross off waivers on August 20. Ross joined the newly acquired Pat Burrell (another guy that no other team wanted) in what was a suddenly crowded outfield. So the lineup kept shuffling, with Bochy constantly looking for the right fit, the right mix, the right complementary parts to his dynamic pitching staff.

With San Diego mired in what would eventually become a ten-game losing streak, the Giants pulled to within three games of the division lead with a 2-1 victory over Ubaldo Jimenez and the Colorado Rockies on September 1st. It marked Lincecum's 12th victory of the year, but more importantly, it was rumored to be the day Aubrey Huff began wearing his legendary red thong. Stuck in a 3-for-32 slump, Huff apparently switched to the girly underwear as a good luck charm. Little did he know, the Giants would be playing the thong song all the way to the World Series.

With all the other playoff positions all but wrapped up, the Giants found them-

NEW ERA
sfgian
NEW ERA
neweracap.com
ankofamerica.com/Giants
bankofamerica.com/Giants
bankofameric

Gibson

Pitching Leaders

Matt Cain
13-11
3.14 ERA

Tim Lincecum
16-10
3.43 ERA

Jonathan Sanchez
13-9
3.07 ERA

Brian Wilson
48 Saves
1.81 ERA

SAN FR

selves in one of the most hotly contested pennant races in recent memory. Fans hung on every pitch as though their lives depended on it. And then, on September 26th, Matt Cain tossed a 3-hit gem in Colorado to move the Giants into first place. After sweeping Arizona, they headed home needing just one win against the Padres to clinch the division. Fittingly, they tortured their fans by dropping the first two games of that series, only to bounce back with a 3-0 victory to win the division in dramatic fashion on the very last day of the season.

The city went wild. Not only because the Giants had made the playoffs for the first time in seven years, but because everyone knew that they had a real shot to do some serious damage. After all, pitching staffs like this one don't grow on trees, and the playoffs are all about pitching. However, amidst the champagne celebration, the same question remained.

Can the Giants score enough runs to win this thing?

55
41

0 0 2
GIANTS
GIANTS

GIA
NTS

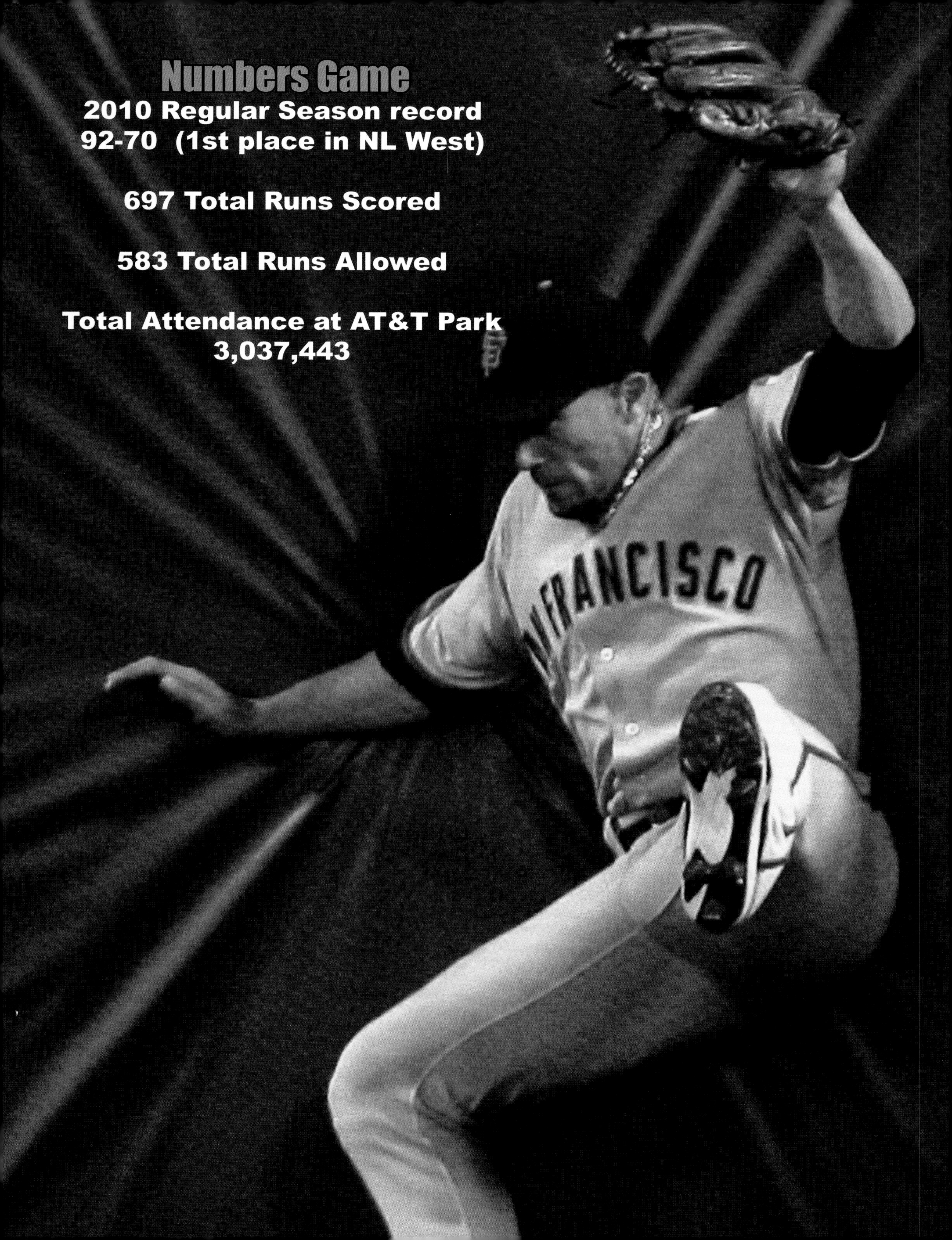
Numbers Game
2010 Regular Season record
92-70 (1st place in NL West)
697 Total Runs Scored
583 Total Runs Allowed
Total Attendance at AT&T Park
3,037,443
FRANCISCO

GUILLEN
6

GIANTS

Fun Facts

• Pitchers Tim Lincecum and Brian Wilson represented the Giants and National League in the Major League All Star Game in Anaheim.

• Giants' collective team ERA (including bullpen) for the month of September: 1.68, the fourth best ERA for any team during any single month since 1920.

• The Giants record from the time Aubrey Huff broke out the thong was 20-10, the exact record Huff predicted in what has become known as the "thong prophecy".

• Buster Posey's real name is Gerald Demps Posey III.

• Andres Torres was the winner of the Willie Mac Award, given to the team's most inspirational player. He spent a dozen seasons in the minor leagues before becoming the Giants everyday lead-off hitter.

• Edgar Renteria became just the fourth player in history to get two World-Series-winning hits in his career (Joe DiMaggio, Yogi Berra, Lou Gherig).

Jonathan Sanchez, on starting the last game of the season:
"I told myself, 'this is my last start and I'm going to win this game.'"

Closer Brian Wilson on the postgame celebration:
"It's been seven years since we've seen something like this. It's been a roller-coaster the entire season."

Pablo Sandoval, commenting on the fact that Giants were in fourth place and 7 ½ games out of first place on July 4th:
"We were in fourth place, but we said, 'we're a team that can win it. We can get to the World Series.'"

Pablo Sandoval on the Giants' total team effort:
"We have one guy hitting a home run one night and another guy hitting a home run another night."

Buster Posey on his hitting streak coming to an end at 21 games, one shy of Willie McCovey's team record for rookies:
"I had fun with it. It would have been something cool to have. But at the same time, I guess in a way it's kind of nice the attention will go back to [the team and winning] instead of the streak."

Willie McCovey on Posey's hitting streak coming to an end:
"He still has time to start another one," said McCovey, noting the season has two months remaining. "So he still might do it."

Making History

Giants vs Braves 2010 NLDS

Giants win 3-1

“It’s been very emotional. Every single pitch. Every single at-bat. Everything was incredible.”
- Cody Ross

With a talented and eccentric cast of characters, the San Francisco Giants entered the postseason on a hot streak and faced the Atlanta Braves in the best-of-five 2010 National League Division Series with one thing on their collective mind: win the first World Series Championship for San Francisco. It was the first taste of October baseball for the Giants since 2003, a campaign in which Barry Bonds was then the face of the franchise. But it only took 119 pitches from the lanky, shaggy-haired two-time Cy Young winner Tim Lincecum to erase the seven-year drought. Before 43,936 screaming, towel-waving fans at AT&T Park, the 26-year-old ace with a tornado of a delivery struck out 14, one short of his career high, in a masterful postseason debut as the Giants beat the Braves 1-0 in Game 1.

Still blistering radar guns with 91 mile per hour pitches in the final inning, the young Lincecum outplayed Braves' veteran Derek Lowe. He went the distance, held Atlanta to two hits and his 14 K's was enough to shatter the franchise postseason record of 10 last accomplished by Jack Sanford in the 1962 World Series.

He had a touch of divine luck to go along with it. The Giants' Cody Ross, a late but vital acquisition in 2010, hit the biggest shot of his life by singling in the only run in the fourth inning after star catcher Buster Posey was called safe on a steal of second in his postseason debut. It was the first career steal for Posey, even though replays showed he was tagged out by Brooks Conrad. What wasn't arguable was Lincecum's pitching clinic, a nearly flawless performance that will be remembered for years to come. He became the first to record 12 strikeouts or more in the playoffs since Roger Clemens had 15 for the Yankees in the 2000 American League Championship Series.

It was a tough night for the Bobby Cox-managed Braves, making their first playoff appearance since 2005, as they played without injured All-Star infielder Martin Prado.

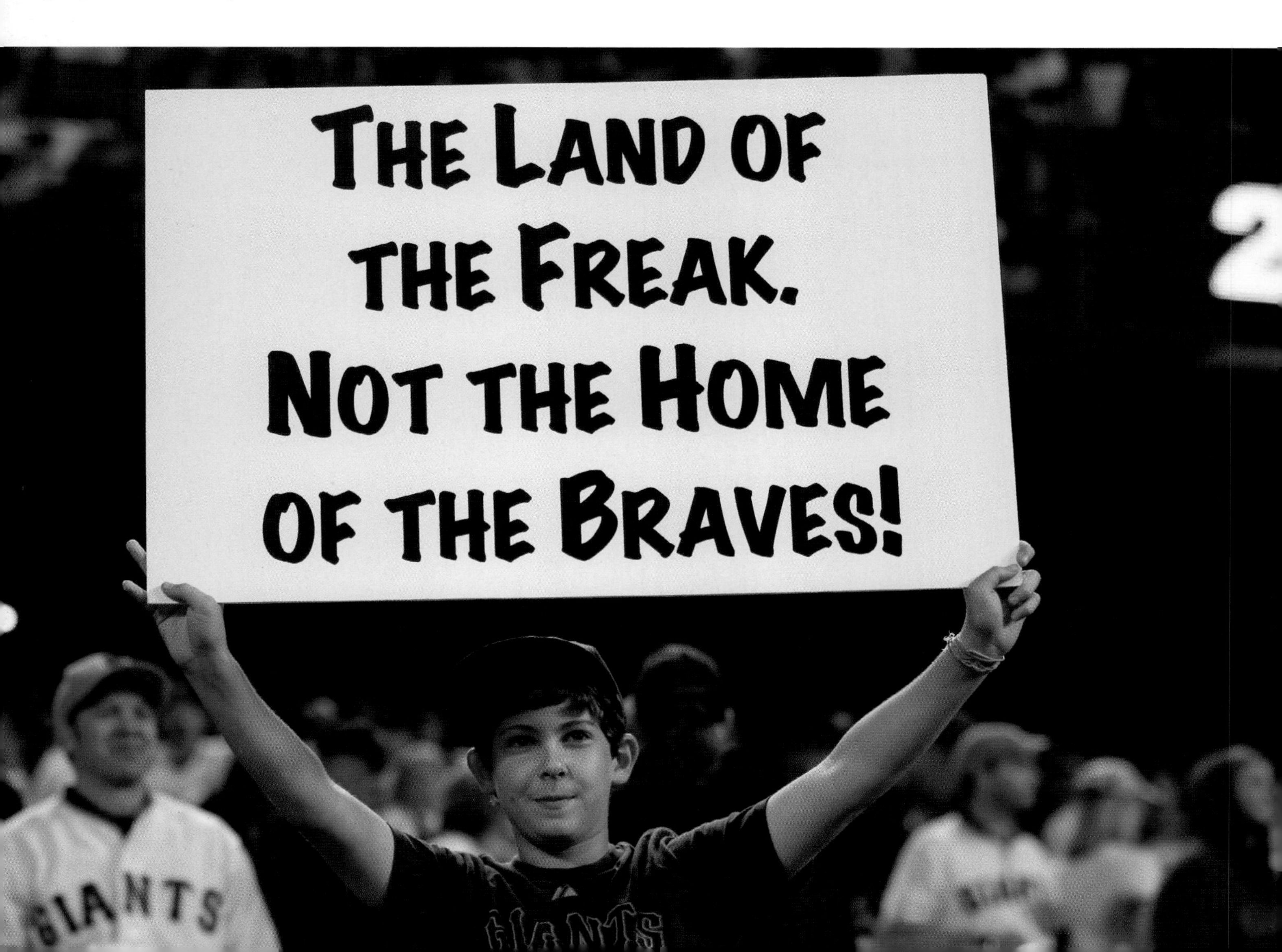

Numbers Game
Tim Lincecum
2 hits
4 strikeouts
Jonathan Sanchez
11 strikeouts
Buster Posey
6 hits
.375 avg
Cody Ross
4 hits
3 RBIs
1 HR
.286 avg
Pat Burrell
2 hits
3 RBIs
1 HR
Omar Infante
4 hits
.222 avg.
Jason Heyward
2 hits
.125 avg.
Derek Lowe
6 hits
4 runs
14 strikeouts
1 HR
October 7 2010
R H E
BRAVES 0 2 2
GIANTS 1 5 0

"As far as shutouts go, I think that was up there with my better ones." *– Tim Linceum on Game 1*

"That's one of the best efforts I've ever seen. What a great job that kid did. He's tough." *- Giants manager Bruce Bochy on Lincecum in Game 1*

"He was lights out. We had two runners at second base all night and that's it."
-- Braves manager Bobby Cox on Lincecum in Game 1

"He struggled so much in August. To be able to do what he's done is a testament to the kid. It was the first time he's really struggled and he came back and manned up." *–Aubrey Huff on Lincecum in Game 1*

Fun Facts

• The last 1-0 postseason game was in Game 4 of the 2005 World Series (Chicago White Sox defeated Houston Astros).

• The last Giants 1-0 win in a postseason game was against the Yankees in Game 3 of the 1923 World Series.

• In Game 1, Lincecum became the first pitcher since 1986 (Mike Scott for the Astros) and sixth in major league history to make his postseason debut with a 1-0 shutout victory.

• Game 1 was the first postseason win since Game 1 of the 2003 division series against Florida, a shutout by Jason Schmidt.

• Lincecum also became the 12th pitcher in history with 14 or more strikeouts in a postseason game.

• Braves manager Bobby Cox watched the final nine innings of Game 2 from the clubhouse after his third career postseason ejection.

In Game 2, Atlanta avoided an 0-2 hole, as two of their newest acquisitions delivered in the clutch. Kyle Farnsworth had a double play in the 10th inning to prevent a rally and veteran Rick Ankiel splashed a home run into McCovey Cove in the 11th as the Braves came back from a four-run deficit to beat the Giants 5-4. Both players joined Cox's club at the trade deadline from the Kansas City Royals. The win may have shifted momentum to Atlanta's Turner Field but if the scrappy, resilient Giants earned anything this season, it was how to come together as a team and deliver in crunch time.

Things started strong as Pat Burrell hit a three-run homer in the first inning to give San Francisco a quick start. From there, each pitch increased the game's intensity, no more evident than when Alex Gonzalez hit a game tying, two-run double in the eighth against 2010 saves leader Brian Wilson. The rally spoiled a stellar postseason debut by Giants starter Matt Cain, who won 13 games this season, but the Braves' league-leading 25 wins in their final at-bat this year was a statistic too difficult to overcome.

"The biggest homer of my career by far. To be honest with you, I wanted to go from the batter's box to the dugout and be with the guys and not run the bases. What a cool thing to do and what a cool way to win." –Rick Ankiel after Game 2 home run

"When I'm called upon, I enjoy being the stopper. When the skipper asks me to come out, regardless of the situation, I feel like I should be able to get out of it. It's already past me. The game's over. I can't really focus on that." – Brian Wilson after Game 2

"It's a tough loss, no getting around it. You have to bounce back. They fought hard. We had a couple of chances to add on, but their pen shut us down." - Bruce Bochy after Game 2

October 8 2010	R	H	E
BRAVES	5	11	0
GIANTS	4	10	2

October 10 2010	R	H	E
GIANTS	3	8	0
BRAVES	2	4	3

Game 3 in Atlanta was tense and emotional for both teams, but even more confounding for one Braves player in particular. His team within one out of taking control of the series, second baseman Brooks Conrad had a night to forget in the annals of playoff baseball. The journeyman, filling in for injured players, made three costly errors, the last of them in the ninth inning on a two-out grounder by Buster Posey that propelled the Giants to a stunning 3-2 victory.

Saves king, Brian Wilson, sporting his trimmed black beard, shut down the Braves in the ninth to secure the Giants' commanding 2-1 lead in the series. With arguably the strongest bullpen in the playoffs, Atlanta's lineup didn't fare well against left hander Jonathan Sanchez, managing only two hits in little over seven innings. The left-hander baffled the Braves with 11 strikeouts and holding them hitless until the sixth. But when pinch-hitter Eric Hinske lined a two-run homer off Sergio Romo in the eighth inning, the Braves suddenly had the lead. Rookie reliever Craig Kimbrel was within one out of chalking up the save before the Giants – characteristically – rallied. Aubrey Huff tied it with a run-scoring single off Mike Dunn. Then, the unflappable Posey hit a grounder right through Conrad.

On an unseasonably warm night in Atlanta, the storied San Francisco Giants quieted a crowd of more than 50,000 to make history of their own with a 3-2 victory in Game 4 that sent them to the National League Championship Series for the first time since 2002. Fitting, of course, that a rookie pitcher and a versatile late-season pickup provided the muscle and all-familiar spark characteristic of the Giants' season.

Sweaty palms and elevated heart rates were the norm for this series -- not likely to be remembered for classic all-around play but for clutch moments by unlikely heroes. Two legendary franchises battled in a series that was tight and tense to the very last out. It was the first in postseason history in which all of the games were decided by one run. The 21-year old Bumgarner became the youngest Giants pitcher to win a postseason game. His teammates didn't let his performance go to waste, even after falling behind twice. Under pressure, Bumgarner pitched six strong innings like a veteran. Atlanta managed just 24 hits in the four games. Derek Lowe did all he could, pitching a no hitter until the sixth inning, but ran out of steam in the seventh. The opportunistic Cody Ross, who entered the game with just two hits in the series, slammed a home run in the sixth to tie the score, and drove in the go-ahead run in the seventh with bases loaded. He grounded a single off reliever Jonny Venters to score Buster Posey with the go-ahead run and give the Giants a 3-2 lead. His late game heroics also helped end the unforgettable career of 69-year-old Braves manager Bobby Cox.

The Giants' bullpen then closed out the game as Santiago Casilla worked almost two innings, Javier Lopez struck out Jason Heyward to end the eighth and Brian Wilson earned his second save in as many nights as Omar Infante struck out on one of Wilson's vintage sliders, and Melky Cabrera grounded out to third. Game over. The stage was set for a marquee clash with the Philadelphia Phillies.

October 11 2010	R	H	E
GIANTS	3	5	1
BRAVES	2	7	2

URIBE
5
16

Fun Facts

• Brooks Conrad had three errors in Game 3, tying a postseason record, done by 11 others.

• The Giants-Braves NLDS is the first series in postseason history in which all of the games were decided by one run.

• The Braves tied a postseason record for errors in a 4-game series with 8, tying the marks previously set by the 1932 Yankees and 2004 Red Sox.

• Madison Bumgarner became the youngest Giants pitcher to win a postseason game, at age 21. He surpassed the previous-youngest, Hal Schumaker (age 22, 1933 World Series)

• Cody Ross singled home the go-ahead run in the 7th inning of Game 4. He is the 4th Giants player batting 8th with a go-ahead hit in the 7th inning or later of a postseason game. The others are Frank Snyder in Game 2 of 1921 World Series, Blondy Ryan in Game 4 of 1933 World Series, and David Bell in Game 4 of 2002 World Series.

• The Giants starters finished with an ERA of 0.93 in the series against Atlanta -- the third-lowest ERA by an NL rotation in a postseason series

tbs
RENTERIA
16

To come back like that after a two-run homer in the bottom of the eighth, I mean, that can take the wind out of your sails. And these guys came right back and found a way to get it done. That is a great win."

"It doesn't feel like the last time I'm putting it on, but it certainly is. I won't put it on again."
–Cox on wearing his uniform for the last time.

"This series had everything. Just the intensity and excitement of the series, it had to be thrilling for the fans. There was never an easy moment for Bobby or myself, because these games could have gone either way."
- Bochy

"I don't know how you can be a fan of this team all year. It's a grind. ... We don't do it easy."
-- Huff

"This isn't the end."
–Posey

"A nice gesture by the Giants. I love (Giants manager Bruce) Bochy. If we couldn't win, I'm glad he did."
–Cox on Game 4 salute from the Giants team

SHOCKING THE WORLD

GIANTS VS PHILLIES 2010 NLCS

GIANTS WIN 4-2

ALL-STAR GAME
TORTURE

Once again, the San Francisco Giants conjured up a dose of magic and got terrific performances from some unlikely heroes. Tim Lincecum followed up his monstrous debut in Game 1 of the divisional series by getting big outs and Cody Ross hit a pair of solo home runs to lead the Giants to a 4-3 victory over the two-time NL Champion Philadelphia Phillies in the series opener. As was becoming the team's modus operandi, the Giants earned their fourth one-run win in the playoffs.

Phillies ace Roy Halladay, who threw the second no-hitter in postseason history in his team's first-round opener, lost his bid for a second one when Ross connected with one out in the third inning. Not showing an ounce of nerves, Lincecum gave up three runs on homers to Jayson Werth and Carlos Ruiz in seven innings but got big outs at critical moments of the game.

San Francisco got two key hits with two outs in the sixth inning, including Juan Uribe's RBI single up the middle, scoring Nate Schierholtz, for a three run cushion, 4-1. Philadelphia quickly answered. Chase Utley nailed a single and Werth hit a two-run shot to right-center to cut it to 4-3. Then, Halladay retired the first seven Giant batters before Ross, a Phillies nemesis, drove a fastball into left center.

All-Star closer Brian Wilson finished with a four-out save.

October 16 2010	R	H	E
GIANTS	4	9	0
PHILLIES	3	7	0

Numbers Game

Tim Lincecum
2 starts
16 strikeouts
3.14 ERA

Buster Posey
5 hits
3 RBI
7 strikeouts
.217 avg.

Cody Ross
7 hits
5 RBI
3 HR
5 strikeouts
.350 avg.

Aubrey Huff
6 hits
3 RBI
.250 avg.

Juan Uribe
3 hits
3 RBI
1 HR
.214 avg.

Freddy Sanchez
9 hits
.360 avg.

Roy Halladay
12 strikeouts,
2 HR
4.15 ERA

Roy Oswalt
14 strikeouts
1.84 ERA

Jayson Werth
2 HR
7 strikeouts
.222 avg.

Chase Utley
4 hits
3 stolen bases
.182 avg.

Ryan Howard
12 strikeouts

"You find out what you're made of. You never expect it to be easy."
– Roy Halladay after Game 1 loss

"I must have a really nice butt. I was hearing a lot of them."
– Tim Lincecum on Philadelphia fans whistling at him during Game 1 victory

In Game 2, the Phillies bounced back to beat the Giants 6-1 on the strength of pitcher Roy Oswalt's arm (and legs) and Jimmy Rollins' four game shifting runs. With the series evened at one, and the Giants managing only four hits in the loss, momentum shifted despite what was to be a celebratory homecoming in San Francisco two days later.

A day after Lincecum outdueled Halladay, Oswalt beat tough lefty Jonathan Sanchez, allowing one run and three hits and striking out nine batters. Sanchez gave up three runs and five hits in six-plus innings. Oswalt also singled and scored a run after racing through a coach's stop sign in the seventh inning, which helped put the game away.

The always dependable Cody Ross hit his third solo homer in two games for the Giants, who struck out 10 times.

October 17 2010	R	H	E
GIANTS	1	4	1
PHILLIES	6	8	0

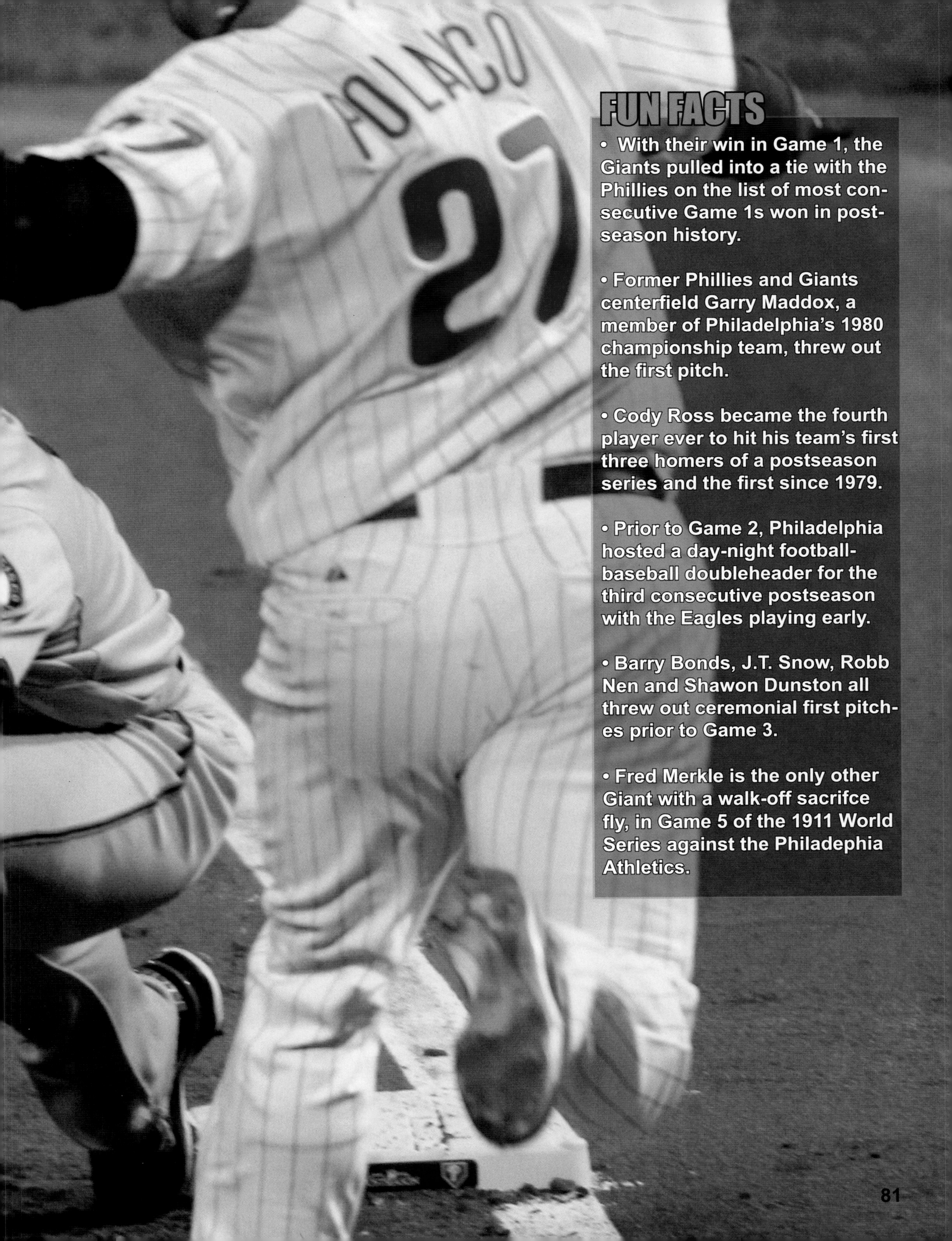

FUN FACTS

• With their win in Game 1, the Giants pulled into a tie with the Phillies on the list of most consecutive Game 1s won in postseason history.

• Former Phillies and Giants centerfield Garry Maddox, a member of Philadelphia's 1980 championship team, threw out the first pitch.

• Cody Ross became the fourth player ever to hit his team's first three homers of a postseason series and the first since 1979.

• Prior to Game 2, Philadelphia hosted a day-night football-baseball doubleheader for the third consecutive postseason with the Eagles playing early.

• Barry Bonds, J.T. Snow, Robb Nen and Shawon Dunston all threw out ceremonial first pitches prior to Game 3.

• Fred Merkle is the only other Giant with a walk-off sacrifce fly, in Game 5 of the 1911 World Series against the Philadepia Athletics.

Phillies

Before a euphoric Bay Area crowd, momentum again shifted in Game 3 and an improbable hero continued to put his stamp on the outcome of this series. With former slugger Barry Bonds cheering him on, Cody Ross delivered again for the Giants. He had homered three times in the first two games at Philadelphia and then hit an RBI single in the fourth inning of Game 3 to break a scoreless tie and Aubrey Huff followed with a run scoring single.

With the victory, the Giants' Matt Cain became the fifth pitcher to throw seven scoreless innings while allowing two hits or fewer in an NLCS victory. He outdueled 2008 World Series MVP Cole Hamels, who didn't allow a hit until Edgar Renteria's single to start the fourth inning, and struck out five in a 119-pitch effort. Chase Utley, Placido Polanco and Raul Ibanez all went 0-for-4 against Cain. Ibanez grounded into a game-ending double play.

Javier Lopez pitched the eighth and Brian Wilson finished the game for his fourth postseason save and second in as many tries this series.

October 19 2010	R	H	E
PHILLIES	0	3	0
GIANTS	3	5	0

One word defined Game 4: charmed. Powered by another big hit from Cody Ross, a memorable four-hit and two-RBI performance from Buster Posey, a double from Pablo Sandoval, and Juan Uribe's sacrifice fly off Roy Oswalt with one out in the ninth inning, the scrappy Giants beat the Phillies in a epic 6-5 battle that gave them a 3-1 series lead. Uribe wound up with the game-winner, leaving the Giants one victory shy of reaching the World Series for the first time in eight years. It was the eighth walk-off sacrifice fly in major league baseball's postseason history.

Jayson Werth's double in the eighth made it 5-all after Ryan Howard doubled against Javier Lopez leading off the inning. Rookie pitcher Madison Bumgarner, who pitched the NLDS clincher at Atlanta, struck out six in just under five innings in his first time facing the Phillies.

October 20 2010	R	H	E
PHILLIES	5	9	1
GIANTS	6	11	0

A champion's heart won't stop easily. A hobbled Roy Halladay's gutsy performance in Game 5 sent the Phillies home with a chance for a third straight NL pennant. He outdueled Tim Lincecum in a 4-2 victory that pulled them within 3-2 in the series. Jayson Werth's solo homer in the ninth, a record 11th in the postseason as a member of the Phillies, quieted the sellout crowd of 43,713.

Halladay allowed two runs and six hits, struck out five and walked two. His bunt also helped spark a three-run third inning, when Shane Victorino drove in the first of two runs. Raul Ibanez snapped his 0-for-15 funk with a single to start Philadelphia's three-run third.

Not lacking for drama, San Francisco put the possible tying run in scoring position in the fourth, fifth and sixth innings but couldn't capitalize.

October 21 2010	R	H	E
PHILLIES	4	6	1
GIANTS	2	7	2

Heading into Game 6, Philadelphia was faced with trying to become the 12th team to rally from a 3-1 deficit in a best-of-seven series. The Red Sox had been the last team to do it, in the 2007 ALCS against Cleveland.

In Game 6, on the road in the hostile city of Philadelphia, the scrappy, unheralded Giants shocked the baseball world, did what most experts thought impossible, and clinched their first trip to the World Series since 2002. Juan Uribe hit a tiebreaking homer off Ryan Madson with two outs in the eighth and the Giants got enough big plays- and big outs - to hold off the defending division champion Phillies, 3-2.

They did it in typical dramatic fashion, too. They overcame a 2-0 first-inning deficit, on an RBI double by Chase Utlety and Jayson Werth's sacrifice fly, tied the game in the third and then went ahead in the eighth when Uribe came up with the big hit. As fans recall, Uribe hit a game-ending sacrifice fly off Roy Oswalt to give the Giants a 3-1 series lead in Game 4.

Tim Lincecum struggled a bit in the eighth, pitching on just one day of rest after a tough Game 5 loss. But Brian Wilson took over and secured the last five outs for his third save of the series, finishing off Philadelphia's bid to become the first NL team in 66 years to win three straight pennants.

October 23 2010	R	H	E
GIANTS	3	13	0
PHILLIES	2	8	1

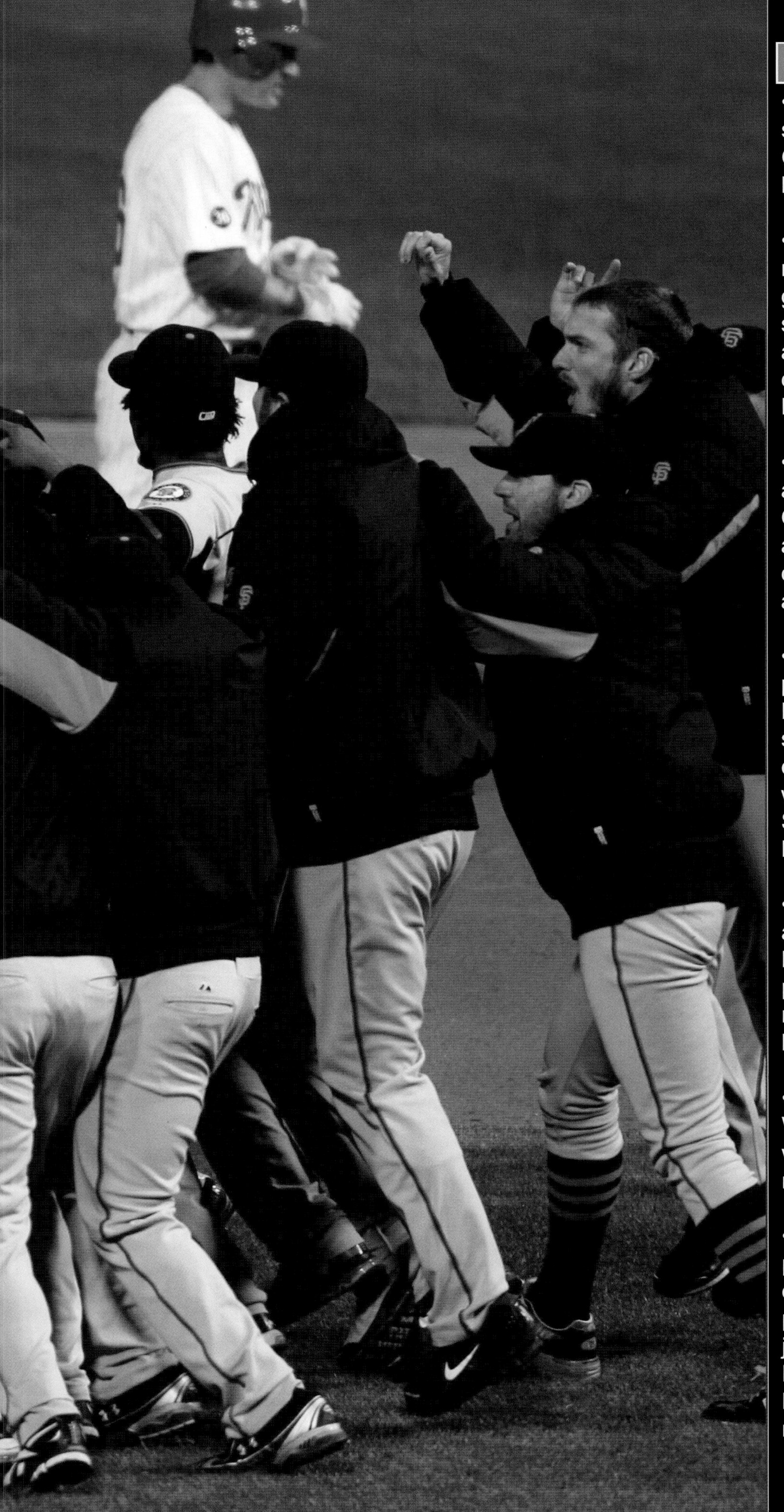

FUN FACTS

• Cody Ross' heroics created signs that included: "Ross for Governor" and "This is Rossto-ber"

• Buster Posey became the first rookie catcher with a multi-RBI game in a postseason game since Geovany Soto (2007 Cubs) and he was the first Giants rookie catcher to have two or more RBI's in a postseason game.

• Prior to Game 5, former Gi-ants Felipe Alou, Jim Davenport, Orlando Cepeda, Willie Mays and Eddie Bressoud all threw out ceremonial first pitches as part of a tribute to the 1958 club.

• Juan Uribe is the seventh player to record a pair of winning RBI's in the same postseason series, with both coming in the eighth inning or later. The last was Joe Crede of the 2005 White Sox. The last NL player was Joe Morgan of the 1975 Reds.

• Philadelphia slugger Ryan How-ard struck out 12 times, tying the LCS record for most in a single postseason, and one shy of the record for any series that he set last year in the World Series.

• The Giants made their 18th World Series appearance, tied with the Dodgers for the 2nd-most all-time.

• In the last 25 years, four NL pitchers have recorded a save of five or more outs to clinch a postseason series. Brian Wilson joins Jesse Orosco (1986 Mets), Randy Myers (1990 Reds) and Byung-Hyun Kim (2001 Dia-mondbacks).

"It's just awesome to be in this situation right now, to be able to come here and help this team where it wanted to be." *– Cody Ross*

"I'm hoping for a momentum switch and get back to San Francisco and take the series there." *– Roy Oswalt*

"It's 1-1, you know? It's tied. We've got to go out there and start winning." *– Freddy Sanchez after Game 2*

"He plays with no fear. That's what you love about the guy." *– Bruce Bochy on Cody Ross*

"He's definitely hot. He's been battling and hitting pitches that most normal people can't hit at this time." *– Cole Hamels on Cody Ross*

"You feel good for them. They're pros. They've done a great job of setting aside their ego. We've got guys who are used to being out there every day. Aaron kept himself ready and gets a start today, gets a big hit, scores a run. They've been a big part of this." *-- Bochy on Aaron Rowand and Edgar Renteria*

"It seems like all the baseball talk is all East Coast. Everybody watching tonight saw exactly how we've played all year." *-- Aubrey Huff following Game 4 win*

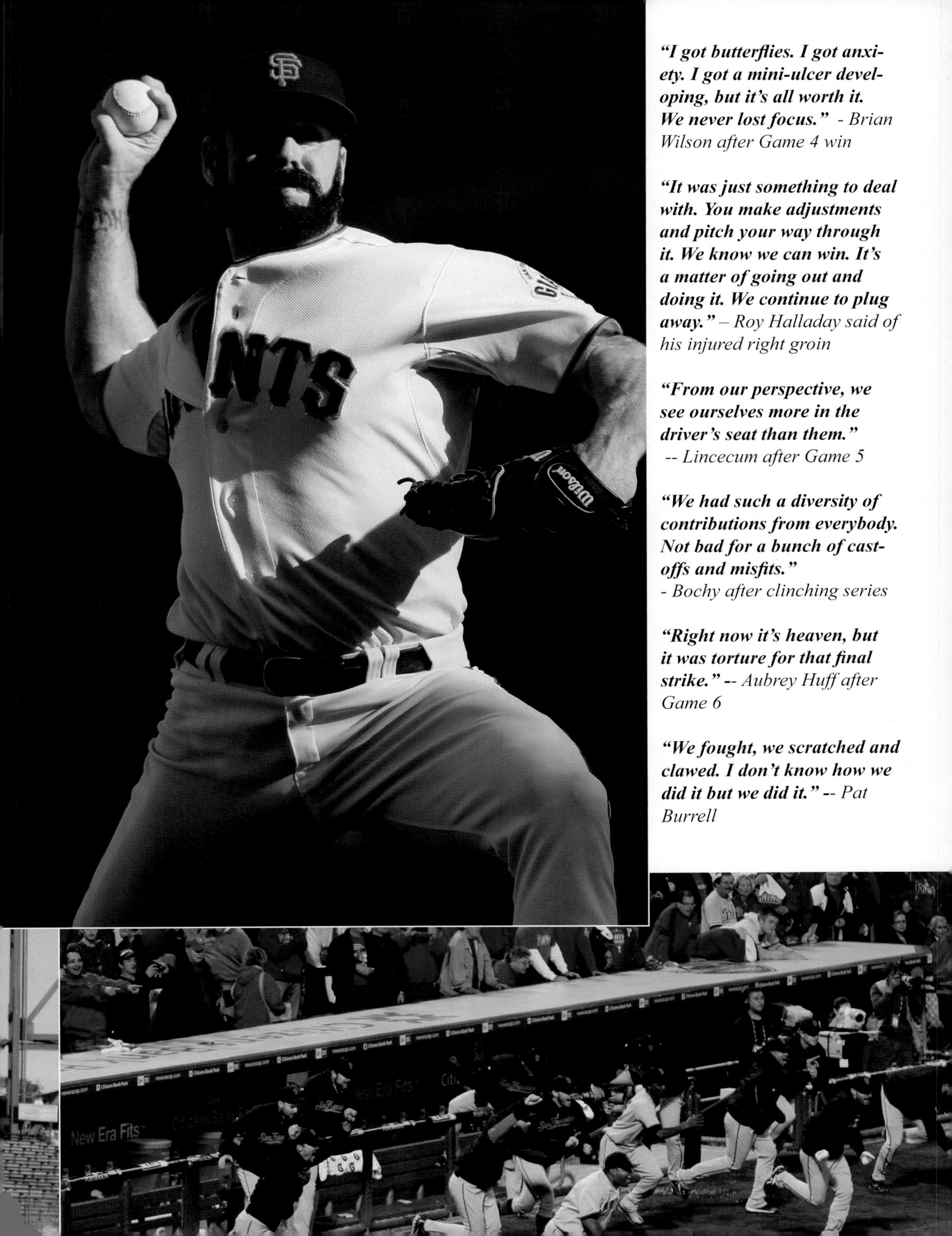

"I got butterflies. I got anxiety. I got a mini-ulcer developing, but it's all worth it. We never lost focus." *- Brian Wilson after Game 4 win*

"It was just something to deal with. You make adjustments and pitch your way through it. We know we can win. It's a matter of going out and doing it. We continue to plug away." *– Roy Halladay said of his injured right groin*

"From our perspective, we see ourselves more in the driver's seat than them." *-- Lincecum after Game 5*

"We had such a diversity of contributions from everybody. Not bad for a bunch of cast-offs and misfits." *- Bochy after clinching series*

"Right now it's heaven, but it was torture for that final strike." *-- Aubrey Huff after Game 6*

"We fought, we scratched and clawed. I don't know how we did it but we did it." *-- Pat Burrell*

Classic Ending

Giants vs Rangers 2010 World Series

Giants win 4-1

Game 1

What a way to start the World Series, as the San Francisco Giants made Cliff Lee look downright mortal. On the game's biggest stage, Freddy Sanchez hit three doubles and sparked a six-run burst in an 11-7 victory in Game 1.

What shaped up as a pitchers' duel between Tim Lincecum and Lee, who came into the game with a 7-0 record, transformed into a rout. By the end, the Rangers made four errors and were left to wonder what went wrong in their inaugural championship series.

Sanchez nailed balls down the sides, Cody Ross and Aubrey Huff hit up the middle and to cap off a dominating performance, Juan Uribe, coming off a couple of big at-bats in the NLCS, launched a booming shot over the wall. The last time the Giants had scored six runs in an inning during the postseason was in the 1937 World Series.

Texas jumped out to a 2-0 lead, but the Giants just as quickly turned things in their favor and it became a blowout. The Rangers chipped away late, scoring three essentially meaningless times in the ninth as Nelson Cruz hit a two-run double off Brian Wilson before the bearded one finished it off.

Sanchez, a former batting champ, finished with four of the Giants' 14 hits, which included six doubles, and Uribe's three-run jolt that broke the game wide open.

The Rangers got eight hits of shaggy haired ace Lincecum, but he walked off the field to a standing ovation in the sixth. All in all, a near perfect way to get things started for the Giants!

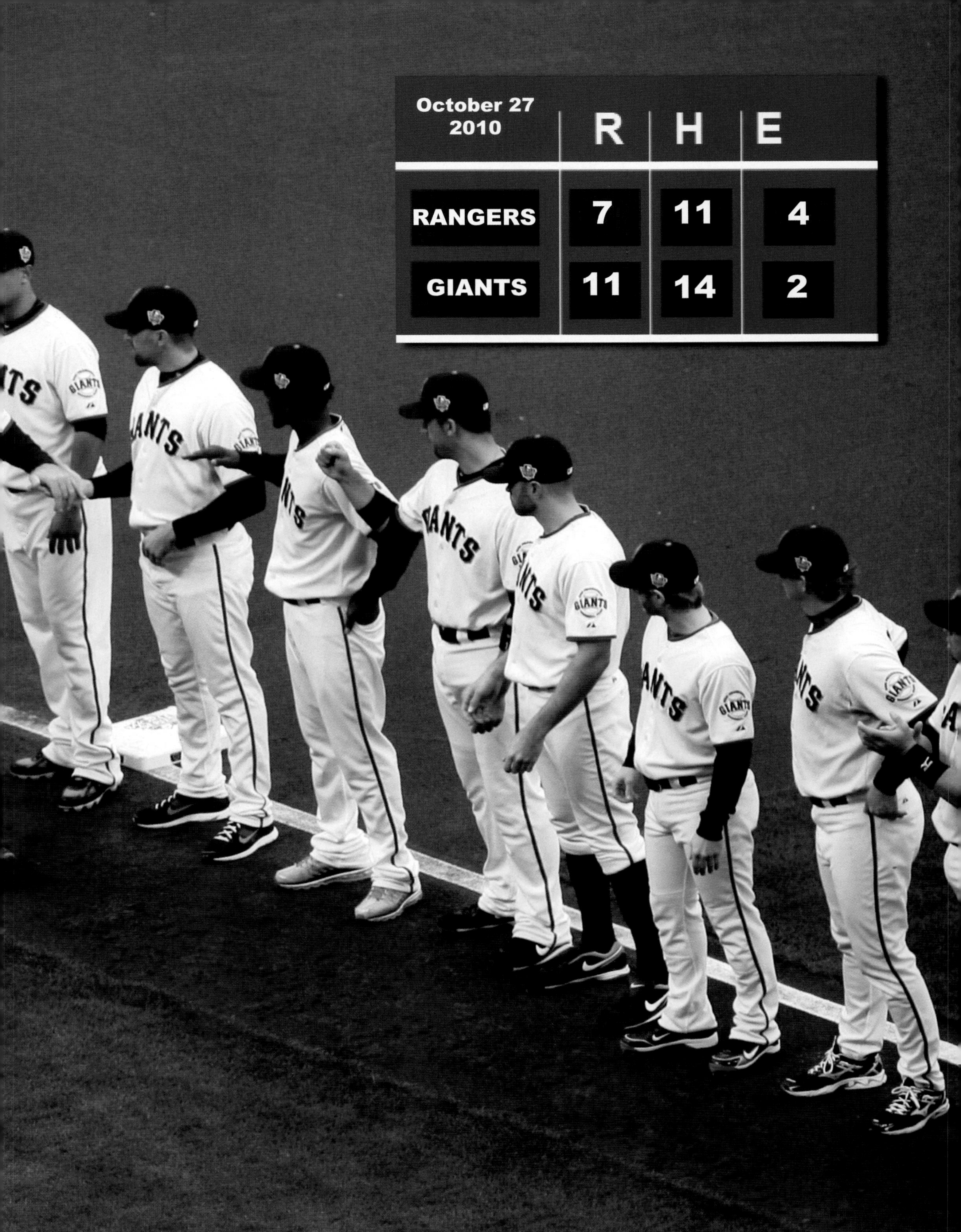
October 27
2010
R H E
RANGERS 7 11 4
GIANTS 11 14 2

Game 2

The Giants continued their dominance in Game 2 with a 9-0 victory and a commanding 2-0 series lead. It was the most lopsided shutout since the 1985 series. Edgar Renteria, whose 11th-inning single won Game 7 of the 1997 Series for Florida against Cleveland, continued his postseason success with a home run and three RBIs. Juan Uribe added a run-scoring single against reliever Darren Oliver.

Texas set a record for most runs allowed in a franchise's first two Series games, a total of 20, which was five more than Colorado did against Boston in 2007.

And as for the Giants offensive explosion, well it would be safe to say it surprised almost everyone, and was literally historic. In fact, San Francisco became the first team in World Series history to score seven runs in an inning after two outs with the bases empty. So after two games it was becoming very clear that the Giants had superior pitching, which everyone knew coming in, but the firepower of their bats is what had the Rangers on their heels. A delirious crowd at AT&T knew in the back of their mind that if things continued, they would not see their team again until a victory parade, and that was more than okay for them. They sent the Giants off the field with a thunderous roar, and what seemed a fantasy this summer, that the Giants could rule the baseball world this season was inching closer to become reality. Destiny was in reach!

Game 3
The Rangers were too good to go down without a fight, and this game certainly did not lack for firepower, although most of it was provided by the two former United States President's named George Bush that were in attendance for the first World Series game in the history of Lone Star State.

On a warm night in Arlington, the Rangers got back in the saddle behind Colby Lewis. They got just enough offense, and plenty of effective pitching to temporarily cool off the red hot Giants and win Game 3 by a score of 4-2, which cut the Giants lead in the series to 2-1.

Rookie Mitch Moreland hit an early three-run homer, Josh Hamilton later launched a 400-plus shot that put the Rangers back in the series and gave them renewed confidence.

As for the Giants, Cody Ross hit a home run in the seventh inning and Andres Torres blasted a solo shot in the eighth, but that would be the extent of the offensive production. The Giants eventually brought the tying run to the plate, but reliever Darren O'Day retired Buster Posey to end the eighth. Lewis picked up where he left off in the division championship series, where he finished off the defending champion Yankees, allowing five hits in more than seven innings and struck out six.

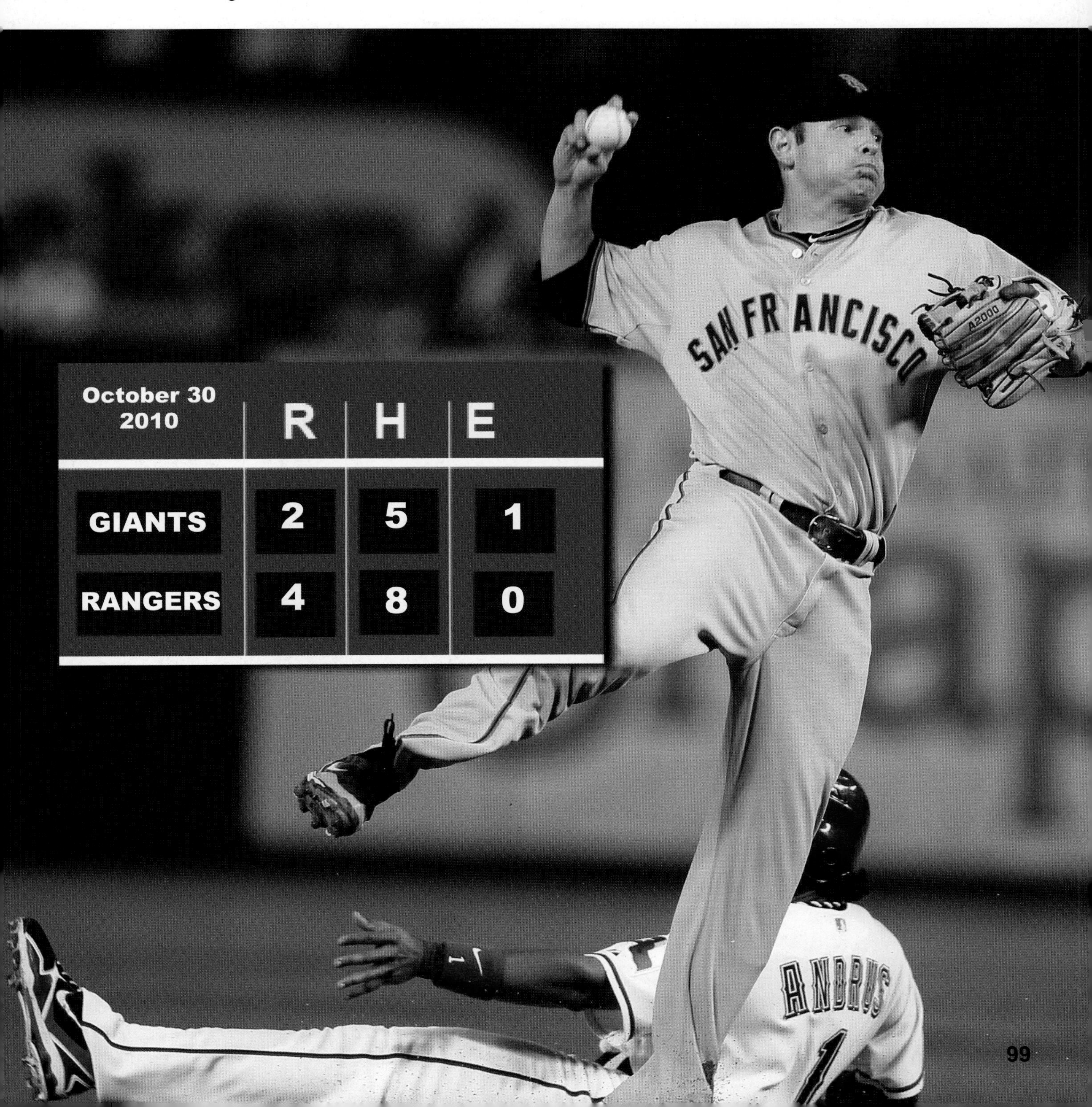

October 30 2010	R	H	E
GIANTS	2	5	1
RANGERS	4	8	0

October 31
2010
R
H
E
GIANTS
4
8
1
RANGERS
0
3
0
RETIRE SUM
CHIKIN
35 Hunter
BOCHY
15
WORLD SERIES
SAN
JCP

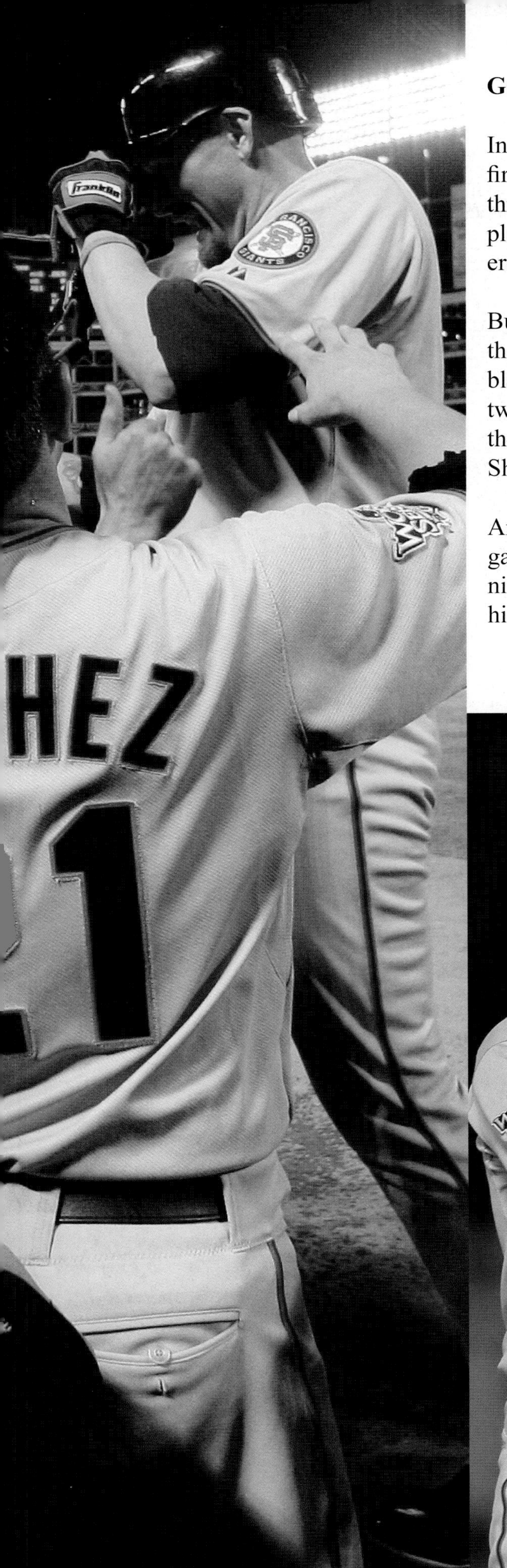

Game 4

In Game 4, everything clicked for the Giants in a 4-0 victory, the first team to post two shutouts in a World Series since Baltimore's three straight against the Dodgers in 1966. Madison Bumgarner played like a seasoned vet and sent a clear message to the Rangers—"we're in it to win it, and we plan on doing it on your field!"

Bumgarner allowed only three hits over eight innings and robbed the sellout Texas crowd of a happy Halloween. The Giants, humbled in Game 3, were aggressive from the start. Aubrey Huff hit a two-run homer in the third and Buster Posey added a solo shot in the eighth, the first rookie battery to start in the Series since Spec Shea and Yogi Berra for the Yankees in 1947.

Andres Torres doubled twice, singled and drove in a run and Edgar Renteria also got three hits. Brian Wilson closed with a hitless ninth. Just like that, the Giants were on the cusp of making baseball history.

MLB.com

Game 5

In Game 5, it became reality and every baseball fan in the world witnessed something truly special. Tim Lincecum, Edgar Renteria and the Giants won the title by beating the Rangers 3-1 in a tense and classic clincher, as the Giants would win their first World Series title since moving to California.

As general manager Brian Sabean said, "This buried a lot of bones -- '62, '89, 2002," recalling the franchise's losing appearances in the Fall Classic. "This group deserved it, faithful from the beginning."

Perhaps no one more than two-time Cy Young winner Lincecum, who outdueled Cliff Lee in a matchup that was scoreless until Renteria earned Series MVP by hitting a magnificent three-run homer with two outs in the seventh inning. Texas' Nelson Cruz homered in the bottom half, but the wily Lincecum preserved the lead. He gave up three hits over eight innings and struck out 10.

Of course it was only fitting that Brian Wilson pitched a perfect last inning for a save, completing a dominating romp through the postseason. Overall, the Giants pitching force shut down Josh Hamilton and the club with the majors' top batting average.

The trophy that eluded so many San Francisco Giants legends was, finally, delivered home and rightfully so by a band of merry men who had just one goal in mind when it all started: win the World Series for themselves and long-suffering Giants fans. As the players stormed the field in a tearful celebration that warmed the hearts of sports fans around the world, this tight-knit group of future Giants legends proved it was mission accomplished!

Final Word

Giants GM Brian Sabean:
"This buried a lot of bones— '62, '89, 2002. This group deserved it, faithful from the beginning. We're proud and humbled by the achievement."

Rangers Manager Ron Washington:
"They beat us soundly. They deserve it."

World Series MVP Edgar Renteria:
"It was a tough year for me, and I appreciate everyone in the organization because they had patience with me -- the GM, the manager. So they gave me the chance to play and thank God everything went well. And I don't know, the home run? I don't know, I saw the ball well, put a good swing on the ball and it went out."

Barry Zito:
"He devastated that lineup. Timmy [Lincecum] was cool as a cucumber out there tonight. I don't even think he threw a curveball. He stayed with his heater and he stayed with his slider. The other side showed that they were on the defensive because they were swinging at the first pitch and they were more aggressive than usual. Timmy took advantage of it."

Cliff Lee:
"You've got to tip your cap to Lincecum. He pitched an unbelievable game. They outpitched us the whole series. Against this lineup, that's highly impressive what they did with the ball. A lot of credit goes to their pitching and defense. It was outstanding, and they flat-out beat us."

FUN FACTS

• The Giants won 6 games this postseason scoring 3 runs or fewer. That ties the 1972 Oakland Athletics for the most wins scoring 3 runs or fewer in a single postseason.

• Tim Lincecum wins his 4th game of the postseason. He passes Christy Mathewson (1905) for the most wins by a Giants starter in a single postseason.

• Edgar Renteria becomes the 5th shortstop to win the World Series MVP.

• Tim Lincecum tied the all-time record for most strikeouts in a World Series-clinching game with 10. He's the first to do it since Bob Gibson in 1967.

• On Wednesday November 3, 2010 the city of San Francisco hosted a victory parade for the Giants. The parade followed the historic route taken by Giant players and coaches to celebrate their move to San Francisco from New York City in 1958.

FUN FACTS

• If World Series MVP Edgar Renteria has played his last game with the San Francisco Giants, he certainly made it a memorable one. The 35-year-old shortstop apparently called his seventh-inning three-run home run that broke a scoreless tie in Game 5 of the World Series on Wednesday night, which the Giants went on to win to wrap up their first world championship.

• In the postgame news conference, Renteria told reporters that, though he has confidence, he "was joking" when he told teammate Andres Torres he was going to hit a home run as he went to the plate. But Torres obviously took him seriously, as he celebrated with teammate Aaron Rowand as Renteria's home run left Rangers Ballpark, screaming "he told me he was going to do it!"

• Brian Wilson became a worldwide celebrity because of his unique, dark, thick beard, but as a pitcher he had an outstanding postseason. He finished the playoffs with six saves, and K'd 16 in 11.2 innings. In the World Series, he allowed one baserunner in 2.2 innings, while striking out four, including Nelson Cruz swinging to seal the Series for San Fransisco.

• The Giants finish the World Series with a team batting average of .249 and a team slugging percentage of .450. The also finished the World Series with a team batting average allowed of .190, and a team ERA of 2.45.

• The San Francisco pitching staff is the first completely homegrown staff to pitch in the World Series since the 1986 Red Sox.

• San Francisco became the second team to clinch three postseason series on the road in one year; the 2005 White Sox also did it, and on that team was current Giants Aaron Rowand and Uribe.

• The last time the Giants won the World Series was as the New York Giants in 1954.Those 1954 Giants were managed by Leo Durocher, and they played in the Polo Grounds. They went 97-57 during the regular season and finished first in the National League, five games ahead of Brooklyn. The team was led by Willie Mays, who hit 41 home runs.

WS

FUN FACTS

• Giants' first baseman Aubrey Huff, who grew up in a Fort Worth-area trailer park with his widowed mother, was a huge Rangers fan in his youth.

• This was only the third time that two teams that train in Arizona have reached the World Series, the first two being the Giants' last two World Series appearances of 1989 and 2002, when they faced the A's and Angels, respectively.

• At 2 hours, 32 minutes, Game 5 was the fastest Series game since Game 4 in 1992 between Toronto and Atlanta, according to STATS LLC

• 12 years ago Giants manager Bruce Bochy and the San Diego Padres were swept in the 1998 World Series.

• The Giants ended the third longest World Series championship drought among major league clubs; their 56-year wait was only shorter than the Cleveland Indians (1948) and Chicago Cubs (1908). They own six titles and have won 49 World Series game; only the New York Yankees (134) and St. Louis Cardinals (52) have won more games in the Fall Classic.

• Tim Lincecum became the 15th pitcher in major league history to win four games in a single postseason. Cliff Lee and Andy Pettitte accomplished the feat last year.

• The National Baseball Hall of Fame took possession of Edgar Renteria's bat and Lincecum's jersey from the clinching victory and plan to display them in the exhibit for the 2010 World Series.

GIANTS

Giants Legend Barry Bonds:

"There is no city that deserves this championship more and I congratulate Bill Neukom, the entire ownership group, Bochy and most of all the guys on the team that fought hard to bring the trophy home to the city of San Francisco. I grew up watching my dad and godfather as Giants, lived out my dream playing in the same uniform in front of the best fans in the world and I just witnessed the Giants winning the World Series. I am ecstatic for the team, the city and all the fans – you truly deserve it."

Giants Legend Willie Mays:

"Oh, man, I don't get overly excited about baseball, but looking at these kids and how excited they were, I

When the Giants last won the World Series:

- I Love Lucy was the #1 show on TV
- Gas cost $0.21 a gallon
- Dwight D. Eisenhower was president
- There were no MLB teams west of the Mississippi

World Series
Game 5 - November 1, 2010

Giants 3
Rangers 1

Relive a night Giants fans have waited over five decades for and will never forget!

WORLD SERIES
SAN FRANCISCO
GIANTS
BASEBALL CLUB

Giants
San Francisco
ECKŌ UNLTD.

San Francisco

CHARLEY PRIDE
PLEASE WELCOME CHARLEY PRIDE
PLEASE WELCOME CHARLEY PRIDE
FRIDAY NIGHT BASEBALL
Snapple

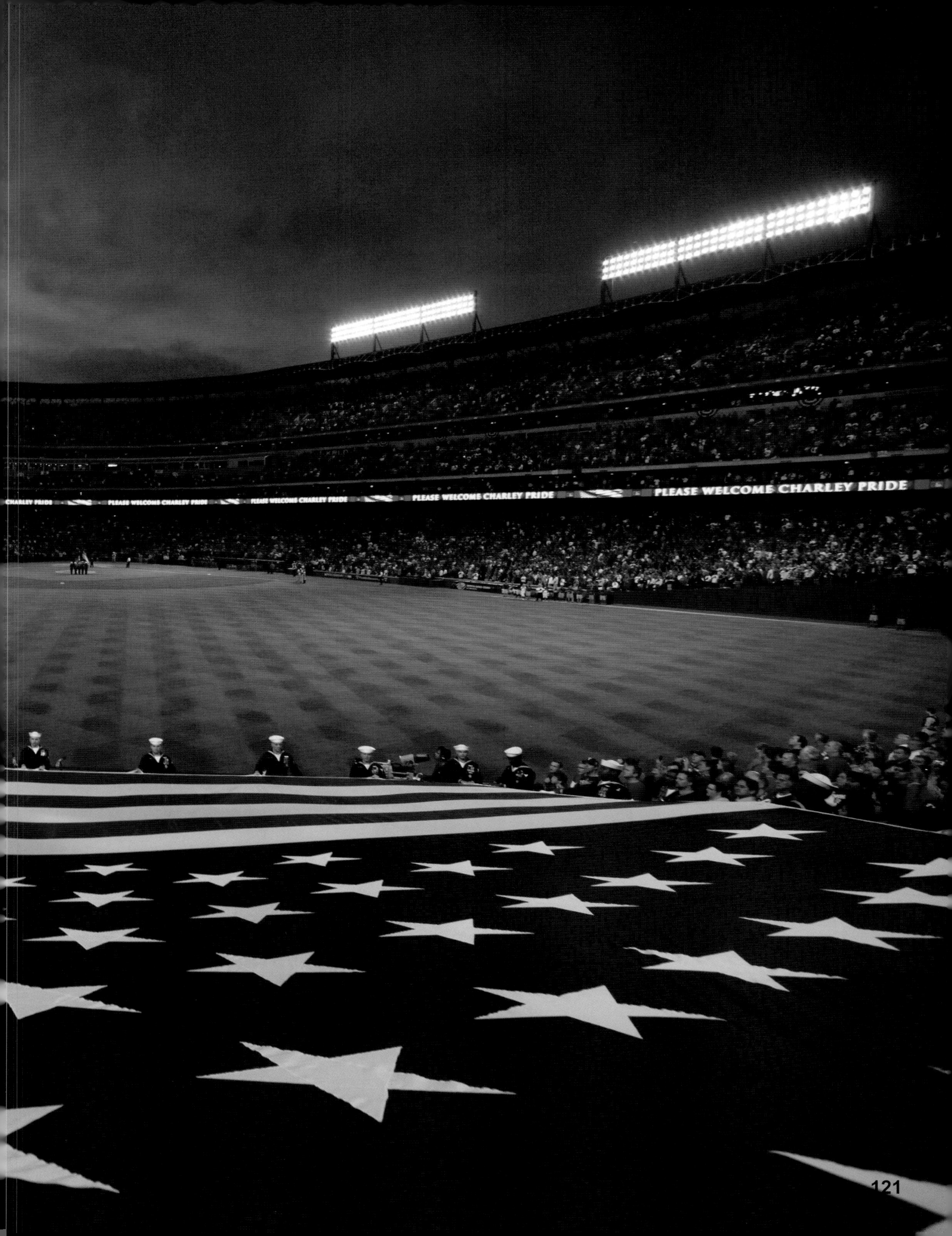
PLEASE WELCOME CHARLEY PRIDE

WILSON
38

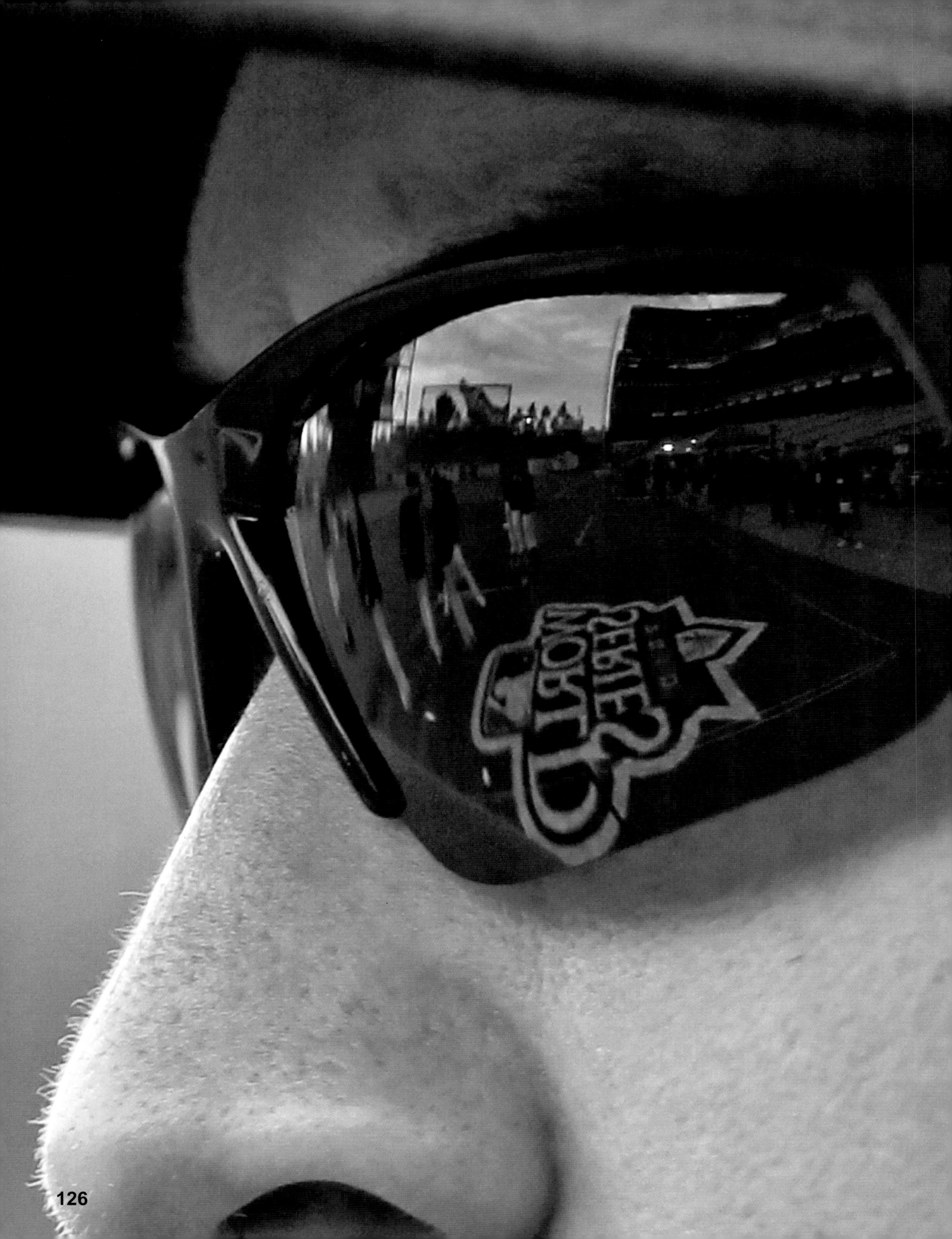

WORLD SERIES
GIANTS

CHAMPIONS

SF

RETIRE SUM
CHIKIN
JCPenney
19

BUD LIGHT
Coca-Cola
WORLD SERIES
9:30
Bud
MSUNG mob!le
12
10
22

GO
TORTURE
ENDS
TONIGHT!
GIANTS
TEXAS

texasrangers.com

WS2010
SERIES

SERIES

THE
DUMP

349
FRIDAY NIGHT
BASEBALL

RIGHETTI
19

WORLD SERIES
FOX

GIANTS

What does it take for team-of-the-ages to re-write history and end a championship drought that had stretched over five decades? Great talent. A shrewd and crafty front office and coaching staff. The loyal support of smart, sophisticated, passionate fans, and of course, some long hair, thick beards and quirky team chemistry that has never been seen in baseball before.

San Francisco welcomed a baseball team to the Bay 52 years ago, and for the first time in 56 years the Giants of the baseball world call San Francisco home. What an amazing ride it was, as a team loaded with a collection of stars, role players, castaways and rising phenoms did what nobody thought would be possible. AT&T Park rocked all summer long, as it took six full months to track down the Padres and clinch a playoff spot, then ride that momentum into the fall in an epic postseason run that saw pitching dominate on a global stage.

It wasn't easy, it wasn't always pretty, but boy, was it beautiful, as for over seven months the Giants leaned on their perfectly assembled collection of history-making players to become the envy of the baseball world.

Enjoy this book as we look back and cherish a remarkable season in which a phenomenal team devoted themselves to their goals and their city, epitomizing what determination and devotion can do when it's combined with exemplary talent—bring home the World Series for the first time since a postage stamp cost three cents and Dwight Eisenhower was president!

$14.95
ISBN 978-0-9831180-1-5
51495>
9 780983 118015

WWW.SFGIANTSWORLDCHAMPS.COM

You'll Never Guess What I'm Saying

Naomi O'Brien